ETHICS in BUSINESS and LABOR

ETHICS in BUSINESS and LABOR

J. Daniel Hess

Introduction by
H. Ralph Hernley

HERALD PRESS
Scottdale, Pennsylvania
Kitchener, Ontario

ETHICS IN BUSINESS AND LABOR

Published simultaneously in Canada by Herald Press, Kitchener, Ont. N2G 4M5
Library of Congress Catalog Card Number: 77-78192
International Standard Book Number: 0-8361-1824-3
Printed in the United States of America
Design: Alice B. Shetler

10 9 8 7 6 5 4 3 2 1

Contents

Introduction

"The County Sheriff expects to receive five hundred dollars in cash if your newspaper wants to continue receiving the advertising from his office," I was told by the previous owner of a newspaper my company purchased. Knowledge of widespread corruption in the county was nothing new to me. But coming into direct contact with this corruption and being forced to make a decision involving the chief law enforcement officer of the county was a real jolt. We lost the sheriff's business!

This is one example of the many kinds of ethical decisions people engaged in business and labor face regularly. Often the pressures are not as blatant as the one related above. They range from practices which are clearly wrong and easy to discern to issues which are hazy and difficult to decide. Other factors may really complicate a decision. For example, if the loss of the advertising income in the illustration above would have forced the owner into bankruptcy, he'd have needed to choose between two unethical consequences. What should be done in such a situation?

Ethical decisions about money or things are usually more clear and less difficult to make than those involving relationships. In the first chapter of *Ethics in Business and Labor* the author points out that most people find it easy to criticize the ethics of others but hard to make decisions concerning their own activities.

Although ethics is an important subject, it is often neglected in Christian circles. Yet ethical decisions need to be made daily. A group of Christian business, professional, and laboring people who had gathered to discuss business relationships were asked, "How many of you have heard a message in your churches during the past year on Christian ethics?" Not one person raised his hand.

Ministers and educational leaders need to give guidance on how to spend money or choose not to spend it, what kind of job a person takes or does not take, whether to sell or not sell a certain product, the decision to purchase or not to purchase an item, how to commend or criticize a fellow worker, one's treatment of an employer or an employee. These and many other situations involve ethics.

J. Daniel Hess is to be commended for the lucid way in which he has organized this subject for group study. Having read a number of books on ethics, I'm pleased to find one that approaches the subject from the viewpoint of both groups—management and labor—working together to solve ethical problems. Few books on ethics have been written with the Christian imperative as the basis for action. There is a real need for more literature on this subject written from a Christian perspective.

In his preface Hess says, "I have tried to communicate that the Spirit of God represents wholeness; when we in business or labor (or any other vocation) live in the Spirit of God, we are at one with each other. The principle of wholeness is supposed to pervade these pages." This is a helpful and Christian approach to the subject of *Ethics in Business and Labor*. The author appeals to basic principles taught in the Scriptures and explores their implications for both management and labor. Chapters divided into purposes, essays, and questions for discussion followed by an activity help the reader face the issues being analyzed. Hess presents the material in a way that will challenge the reader and the group to respond in action.

Ethics in Business and Labor will be helpful in a variety of settings. It can be used as a Sunday school or Bible school elective or as the focus for small classes organized specifically to study the subject. It can be used in business by employers and employees to help them obtain a clearer understanding of opposing viewpoints.

The Mennonite Industry and Business Associates (MIBA) organization helped subsidize this book because we recognize the importance of the issues discussed. One of the purposes of MIBA is "to help Christian business and professional people to discern and establish criteria for Christian ethical relationships." This book will be a definite asset in helping to meet this purpose. Local groups associated with MIBA will find it an excellent resource for guidance and for programs. This book may be used as a text in schools where the students are old enough to have had some work experience.

Although Hess writes from a Mennonite background, *Ethics in Business and Labor* is adaptable to the use of all Christian people. His viewpoint is based on teachings in the Scriptures and is not denominational in nature.

H. Ralph Hernley, President
Mennonite Industry and Business Associates, Inc.

Author's Preface

Two unfortunate attitudes are sure to emerge whenever Christian people discuss business and labor ethics. The first attitude rides on words such as these: "The church should keep its nose out of my business, and I should not bother the church with my private affairs." I disagree. One's faith *and* one's business should be of equal concern to the fellowship of Christian believers.

The second attitude prompts Christian people to want to talk about money and finances and employment, but to do it with careless and accusatory generalities, with illogical thinking, heated emotion, and flippant moral demands. Said one Christian brother, "Every month or so we get into one of these harangues about business, as though we had to exorcise some mercenary demon inside us. Then quieted, we go about our Monday business as usual." Christian people should discuss business and labor ethics with the same care as they discuss mission strategy or doctrinal statements.

These two attitudes have perplexed me, so when I was asked to study and write on this topic, I said yes on the very first phone conversation. I was not given the assignment because I am a manager or a laborer. Nor am I an ethicist or a theologian. (I wish I could present here a systematic theology and ethic for the Christian entrepreneur and the Christian laborer. We need that badly.) I was asked to write because someone thought I might chronicle the consciences of people around me who want the claims of the gospel to matter a lot more than they now do. So what you have here is a study guide in which you will encounter many Christian people, their questions, and their answers.

Leadership for this project was provided by a Task Force on Business and Labor Problems, established by the Mennonite Board of Congregational Ministries. Task Force members suggested lesson titles, subject matter, readings, and areas of most tension. They also read the manuscript draft and gave many suggestions for the revision.

It is possible to work through this study guide in the privacy of a living room. But the material was prepared primarily for the church and would best be studied in community in a Sunday school class, a prayer group, a youth fellowship. The way to get the most from these resources is make use of the questions for discussion, the recommended activities, and the references for further study following each essay.

If this book shows a pro-management or a pro-labor bias, such was not my intent. I have tried to communicate that the Spirit of God represents wholeness; when we in business or labor (or any other vocation) live in the Spirit of God, we are at one with each other. The principle of wholeness is supposed to pervade these pages.

J. Daniel Hess
May 1977

CHAPTER ONE

The Divide in the Church

Purposes

A. To discover why business persons and nonbusiness persons become separated in the church.

B. To assess the damages sustained by the church when its members divide.

C. To identify some initiatives to be taken by both business persons and nonbusiness persons to bridge the chasm between them, thus restoring integrity to the church.

Essay

The Beacon Light Sunday School class had just concluded a particularly intense discussion on wealth. What had begun as a study of stewardship, based upon Jesus' baffling statement, "Do not store up for yourselves treasure on earth . . ." (Matthew 6:19) had turned into a somewhat focused disagreement about a certain "line" of business.

One of the sixteen class members struck the match: "I couldn't be a Christian so long as I was a slum landlord, charging top rents for run-down shacks." Flames shot up from nearly everyone. About the only quiet class member was a 37-year-old man who, to the knowledge of everyone in class, owned twenty-some apartment units in town.

After class, in fact hours later, this apartment owner reflected on the class discussion. "Since I've gone into business, I've felt strange reactions from church members. People seldom speak directly to me about my apartments, but quite often I'm hit by these indirect attacks that imply I'm unethical. The question has crossed my mind, why continue going to church?"

There it is—the chasm between business and nonbusiness people in the church. Who are the people on either side? Managers and laborers may be easy to categorize but many persons such as teachers, salespeople, housewives, and artists, do not neatly fit into either group. However, for purposes of discussion we will outline two sets of attitudes.

A. The Chasm

A chasm is a deep cleft, a yawning fissure, an impassable ravine, a gap, a gorge, a canyon that separates the structure of the earth. Such cleavages can separate people as well. When the people on one side look across the chasm at people on the other side the picture they see is sometimes not very accurate.

What is the picture of business as seen by nonbusiness persons from across the chasm? In the words of a non business person:

1. *Business today is generally unethical.* National news coverage of payoffs, illegal political contributions, collu-

sion in price-fixing, deceptive advertising, padded expense accounts, pollution, false public relations claims—all bespeak corruption. Even executives themselves—four out of five in a *Harvard Business Review* study[1]—confirmed the presence of practices in their industry which are generally accepted but are clearly unethical.

2. *The chief goal of business is profit.* Even though a bank's brochure may claim that "City Bank was founded to protect your funds," we know that its wealthy directors run the bank to make money for themselves and for stockholders. A first reward in the capitalistic, private enterprise system is profit (with all the rights and privileges that profit brings.) The higher a person climbs in an organization, the more money and recognition he expects.

3. *Business power and authority are destructive.* Lord Acton said, "Power tends to corrupt and absolute power tends to corrupt absolutely." The business person who has power to hire and fire, to set salaries, to establish prices, to make decisions that affect an entire community, to boss a secretary will quickly lose the capacity to be admonished by the church.

4. *Society discriminates in favor of the rich.* If indeed we are equal under God, we certainly aren't equal under social custom. Tax laws with their depletion allowances, interest deductions, capital gains provisions, and mortgage exemptions obviously favor rich people. Many clubs and recreational facilities can be afforded only by the rich. The courts are known to be biased: even a national leader recently questioned why big-shot crooks should go free and the poor ones go to jail.

5. *Business fosters an objectionable style of living.* "The spread between rich and poor [is] driving a wedge in our communities," wrote Calvin Redekop, after interviewing Christian business people throughout the United States and Canada.[2] How can a person who lives in a house triple the value of mine, who drives a luxury car, takes expensive vacations, eats in exclusive restaurants be comfortable in my house, in my car, on our porch swing, at our table? How can a business person, so very very busy, stop long enough to talk with me?

6. *Scriptures are anti-business.* How often Jesus warned against riches! "It is easier for a camel to pass through the eye of a needle than for a rich man to enter the kingdom of God" (Mark 10:25). The Apostle James concurs: "Has not God chosen those who are poor in the eyes of the world to be rich in faith and to inherit the kingdom?" (James 2:5).

This picture of the business person isn't complimentary, is it? On the other side, the picture of the nonbusiness person, as seen from across the chasm, is no more complimentary. The business person might say:

1. *Nonbusiness persons make poorly-informed judgments.* They do not understand the variety of worthy motives for being in business, the risks of investment, the need for capital to begin and maintain a business, the dynamics of supply and demand on the market, the pressures to pay bills, the heavy responsibilities of administering people. Nonbusiness people would hardly accept amateur opinions in their own specialties, yet they freely tell us how to do our work.

2. *Nonbusiness persons don't adequately appreciate the free-enterprise capitalistic system.* Influenced by

liberal social critics, theory-oriented political philosophers, left-wing theologians, and even church administrators, the nonbusiness people not only are criticizing the free enterprise system which has produced one of the world's greatest societies, but also are favoring legislation that further limits independent entrepreneurship. Some professors, missionaries, and writers go so far as to advocate socialistic systems.

3. *Nonbusiness people isolate those in business leadership.* An acquaintance of a community's most wealthy and influential leader said, "He has few friends. His former ones have forsaken him, possibly from fear. Those who now call on him come asking for a favor; he naturally pulls back. He is one of this community's loneliest people."

4. *Nonbusiness people express disapproval, seldom approval.* They are not discriminating enough to notice how my business practice differs from the next person's. When they do notice, they say nothing. The housewife is complimented for her good meal, the schoolteacher for good classroom atmosphere, the doctor for an effective prescription, but we hear nothing when our pricing puts us at a competitive disadvantage, when we expend a lot of energy helping an employee whom others would dismiss, when we suffer reduced sales by closing shop to help in a church function.

5. *Nonbusiness people expect us to "bail them out."* No matter how irrelevant or even unethical we may appear to the church, its treasurer has no hesitancy to come when the church needs money. It's a strange alienated feeling—the church peeking into my pockets without looking at my face.

6. *Nonbusiness people disregard our skills.* Our so-called classy style of living might be a result not of selfishness, but of effective financial management. We may pay less for food, clothing, and transportation—even housing—than do nonbusiness people. Yet these skills in handling money are neither recognized as God-given talents, nor requested for the work of the church.

B. A Church Divided

A church divided has lost its integrity—that quality of being whole. To make an undivided body was Jesus' object in coming to earth. He prayed, "Holy Father, protect by the power of thy name those whom thou has given me, that they may be one, as we are one" (John 17:11). A brief glimpse of what Jesus intended is described in Acts 4:32. "The whole body of believers was united in heart and soul. Not a man of them claimed any of his possessions as his own, but everything was held in common, while the apostles bore witness with great power to the resurrection of the Lord Jesus."

A church that has lost its integrity can hardly be a unified voice of prophecy, a hand of healing, a circle of fellowship, a congregation of worship. Some churches, like social clubs, become cliques of people with similar biases of color, profession, academic level, economic status, or political persuasion. The ministry of such churches is broken also.

While one expects a beautiful diversity of gifts in the church, one should not find the destructive divisions of Jew against Gentile, slave against master, rich against poor, male against female, white against black, Western against Eastern, professional against nonprofessional, white collar against blue collar, adult against child.

When a gap separates business persons from nonbusiness persons what more precisely is the nature of the damages? At one level, the damage is personal and psychological. Dr. Abraham Maslow[3] has pointed out that persons need to be creative and their desire to serve others cannot be satisfied until more basic "hunger needs" are met. One such basic need is for a sense of belonging, of affiliation. If a member of the church cannot satisfy this urgent hunger, the alienated person may turn elsewhere—to other people or to other gratifications. No longer "your people shall be my people, your God my God."

At another level, the chasm between business and nonbusiness persons damages the church's mission. The church, in any one era, is called to address particular needs such as refugee relief, disaster relief, mental health services, education, senior citizen services, and a witness against war. Today the creativity of the church ought to be focused on business issues: the development and distribution of resources in a world of finite resources, the prophetic witness against economic principalities and powers which harbor an evil commerce. But with what vigor can the church create and with what clarity can it prophesy when the church hasn't yet brought together its own business and nonbusiness members?

C. A Reunion

"Going the second mile," when a chasm lies immediately ahead, means that the traveler must be a bridge builder. Through what kinds of initiatives can both the business and nonbusiness persons build bridges?

1. Education. A bias is difficult to modify, especially when it is fed by ignorance. Ignorance abounds concerning business and labor. Business persons should not be hesitant to describe the details of an eroding credit base, the drama of a rapidly expanding market for a new product, the trauma of pressures from a faltering retail outlet, the frustration of a large accounts receivable.

The laborer should not hesitate to describe a workday, the factory atmosphere, relationships with the boss and crew, the struggle to live on $150 a week, the shock of being laid off, the fulfillment resulting from good workmanship. Those in occupations not usually categorized "business" or "labor" should likewise help their sisters and brothers to learn of their employment.

From this education will come appreciation, particularly for new gifts heretofore unrecognized in the fellowship: the ability to perceive opportunity, the ability to marshal resources, the ability to make contact in the community, skills in personnel management, expertise in accounting, knowledge of the manufacturing process, familiarity with legal processes, gifts of creativity, endurance, patience. Heretofore, the definition of "gift" has been too limited.

Appreciation will come also when people learn to share each other's burdens. Life may be easy when operations are routinely covered by policy. But "the times that try men's souls" are those when choices must be made between conflicting values, when decisions affect human welfare, when our actions determine long-range effects on others.

2. Repentance. Bring aliens together before the presence of God, and they will want to fall down in repentance. So it is with business and nonbusiness people. More than likely the confessions will recognize the failure to fear God as the Creator of life and the Lord of our industry, the selfishness that makes us want to reap large profits, the avarice that causes us to grab for goods and services, to fight for every benefit, to struggle to be the Joneses that others will want to keep up with. And the confessions will beg God and our brothers and sisters for forgiveness for those occasions when we abuse our talents, decline opportunities, remove ourselves from the difficult issues of development, and refuse to do our job well. And finally, the confessions will recognize the harshness with which we judge others and the lack of information that prompts us to condemn their motives.

3. *Communion.* The church should be strong enough to be the place to share a confidence, the atmosphere to receive counsel, the location to distribute the heavy burden a member is carrying, the moment to celebrate a success, the source of new energy and vision. This is communion at its deepest level.

When people of varying gifts and constrasting authorities can wash each other's feet, each person can come to an enriched sense of self-worth, autonomy, and responsibility. Those who have experienced mutual aid—either in giving or receiving—knows its power to unite and strengthen a people.

4. *Bible study.* The Scriptures say a lot about money and stewardship, but we have too often violated the message by using isolated verses as missiles to send to the other side of the chasm. "One can make the Bible say anything," is a good warning to us.

We need more methodical and diligent study of the

entirety of the gospel message—the context in which it was given, the larger purposes of God in history, the meaning of the life and ministry of Jesus, and the work of the Holy Spirit in a living community of faith. Only with this larger perspective can we perceive the fullness of Scriptures.

5. *Mission*. Too much self-analysis and introspection can be self-defeating. Instead of suspecting each other, we should work together at the church's mission and in that selfless effort find healing. What that mission is deserves at least enough rephrasing to involve our occupations: to be stewards of our salaries, to love our competitors, to make disciples of those we work with; to give witness to the kingdom of God even among the powers of economic systems; and to demonstrate personal integrity in complex organizational life. Our mission includes modesty in handling power, fairness in matters of human rights, restraints in profit-taking, and clarity in the priority of values.

The chasm is not inevitable. The church can have its wholeness. The grace of God is available.

Questions for Discussion

1. Do all business people need to bend ethical standards to survive?

2. If your company had to lower specifications to survive—without changing the advertising labels—would you be willing to do it?

3. Do you know of two families with widely different incomes who get along well? How do they build good relationships?

4. Do you appreciate inquiries about your job or busi-

ness from church members?

5. What are some of the remarks that most hurt you in your job or business?

6. Can you think of a law that favors you over someone else in the congregation?

7. What is "profit"? Discuss the difference between "profit-taking" and "recapitalization." When is profit excessive? When is profit insufficient?

8. Should a church member go into business with someone who is not a Christian?

9. Should the church provide an agency to make loans to members, counsel families with their budgets, participate in labor negotiations, give opinions on land development, perform business "audits," and serve as a forum for business misunderstandings?

An Activity

Prepare a profile of someone you think is on the other side of the chasm from you. If you are in business, select a nonbusiness person; if you are not in business, select a business person. Ask him/her for a coffee conversation. Here are some questions you might ask:

1. What is one difficult work-related decision you made this month?

2. Describe one of your skills.

3. Tell of specific ways you exercise authority. In turn, who are the authorities that place limits upon you?

4. If you were "starting over," what would you do differently?

5. Name two goals you hope to reach in the next five years.

6. Does the church have any business becoming in-

volved in the issues you face in your vocation?

Report back to the class what you have learned. Be sure to tell the person you are interviewing that you will be sharing the conversation with others, and if the interviewee requests a confidence, respect it.

References for Further Study

A. From the Bible

Acts 4:32—5:12 (a vignette of a unified church).

B. From church periodicals

William Keeney, "Christian Ethics in Business and Professions," *Mennonite Life*, December 1972.

John H. Rudy, "Money Talks! What's It Saying About You?" *Gospel Herald*, September 21, 1976.

C. From religious textbooks

Harold S. Bender, *These Are My People* (Herald Press, 1962).

C. Norman Kraus, *The Community of the Spirit* (Eerdmans, 1974).

D. From books about ethics

Raymond Baumhart, *An Honest Profit: What Businessmen Say About Ethics in Business* (Holt, Rinehart & Winston, 1968).

E. Other sources

During the weeks of this study, read carefully the items about business in your local newspaper or weekly newsmagazine.

CHAPTER TWO

Lessons from the Past

Purposes

A. To summarize themes from the Bible that establish foundations for ethical living.

B. To identify principles for ethical business practice from the heritage of the church.

Essay

Is the Bible relevant to this topic of business/labor? We imagine the typical Bible setting: a traditional village of seventeen or eighteen white, flat-roofed houses; barefoot children arguing rules of their game within earshot of village ancients who lean on canes; a well from which women draw a day's supply of water and gossip; craggy hills where boys reluctantly trudge after their father's sheep; shopkeepers haggling over the final sale prior to the midday break. Can the Bible, emerging from its 2000-year-old dust, speak with authority on modern business practice?

The Scriptures should not be regarded as an economics textbook, but they may be compared to a sacred symphony in which themes are announced and developed by many writers in differing eras and in contrasting circumstances—themes that give form to our understanding of Christian behavior in a dusty, primitive hamlet or in the executive headquarters of a multinational corporation.

A. Three Themes from Scriptures

1. Jehovah has a purpose. The Lord God, the Beginning and the Ending, the Creator and Sustainer of life, is the purpose of our lives. A rich development of this theme is provided from Job's early testimony, "I know that thou canst do all things and that no purpose is beyond thee" (Job 42:2) to Paul's exclamation, "O depth of wealth, wisdom, and knowledge in God: How unsearchable his judgments, how untraceable his ways!" (Romans 11:33).

God, the purposeful Initiator, gives meaningful assignments to people: "Be fruitful and increase, fill the earth and subdue it, rule over the fish in the sea, the birds of heaven, and every living thing that moves upon the earth" (Genesis 1:28).

People are held individually accountable for their stewardship: "Where a man has been given much, much will be expected of him" (Luke 12:48).

Only when the purpose of God is the noun and predicate, the object and modifier of our industry can we realize the perfect will of God. Writes Arthur Campbell Ainger:

God is working His purpose out
  As year succeeds to year:
God is working His purpose out,
  And the time is drawing near;

Nearer and nearer draws the time,
The time that shall surely be,
When the earth shall be filled with the glory of God
As the waters cover the sea.

All we can do is nothing worth
Unless God blesses the deed;
Vainly we hope for the harvesttide
Till God gives life to the seed;
Yet nearer and nearer draws the time,
The time that shall surely be,
When the earth shall be filled with the glory of God
As the waters cover the sea.[1]

2. *Jesus builds a kingdom.* Jesus, the Author of the constitution of the Kingdom, teaches us to pray, "May thy kingdom come." The prayer strengthens our desire, for the admission standards are extraordinarily rigorous: "If anyone wishes to be a follower of mine, he must leave self behind; day after day he must take up his cross, and come with me" (Luke 9:23).

The Bible refers often to people in occupations—farming, orcharding, fabrics, fishing. Most references to the occupation are neutral in tone. But Jesus, in announcing the kingdom, calls people away from any earthly commitment and into a singular allegiance to God. "No servant can be the slave of two masters; for either he will hate the first and love the second, or he will be devoted to the first and think nothing of the second. You cannot serve God and Money" (Luke 16:13). This all-or-nothing standard caused Jesus, in some cases, to ask a business entrepreneur to sell out. It prompted Him on occasion to ask laborers to leave their jobs.

3. *Justice is fulfilled in love.* A third theme pertains to

God's sure judgments and His corresponding insistence upon justice on earth. "Do what is right and just," urges a proverb, "that is more pleasing to the Lord than sacrifice" (Proverbs 21:3).

God's laws to the people of Israel made of justice an imperative far stronger than mere suggestion. "You shall not be led into wrongdoing by the majority, nor, when you give evidence in a lawsuit, shall you side with the majority to pervert justice; nor shall you favour the poor man in his suit" (Exodus 23:2).

Jesus rescued justice from becoming an impossibly detailed legal maze. His concern for justice was a peculiar one, writes Professor John Redekop. "It is primarily a concern to do justice and only secondarily a concern to obtain justice."[2] A concern *to do* justice leads inevitably into the love ethic.

The new ethic confounded even the specialists in justice when Jesus said things such as, "The spirit of the Lord . . . has sent me to announce good news to the poor, to proclaim release for prisoners and recovery of sight for the blind; to let the broken victims go free, to proclaim the year of the Lord's favour" (Luke 4:18, 19).

Herein is salvation—that Christ would deliver people from the bondage of evil, so that they in turn could carry justice and love to others.

Agape love, leading to social justice, is the topic of hundreds of Bible verses related to the lending of money (Luke 6:32-36), greedy expansionism (Luke 12:13-21), master-servant relations (Colossians 3:22—4:1), accumulation of wealth (Matthew 6:19, 20), settling of business disputes (1 Corinthians 6:1-11), and economic discrimination (James 2:1-7). But in studying them, consider the larger context within which the verses fit.

B. Church History

What's a religious heritage for? Just as we opened this essay with questions about the relevance of ancient Scriptures for contemporary life, so we ponder the significance of one's more immediate religious heritage.

In modern times, we assume that we'll survive our problems by using a temperate mixture of intelligence, common sense, and technology. We are naive. One can't "mix up" a batch of wisdom. Rather, we search for it, "as for hidden treasure." That search leads us to study the total experience of humanity as the revelation of God and sends us slowly, carefully, and somewhat reverently back into history. That's what a heritage is for.

We shall search through one particular heritage—the Anabaptist-Mennonite tradition. Readers who are not members of that tradition, are encouraged to let the Anabaptist-Mennonite experience spark reflections upon their own religious heritages.

The Anabaptist-Mennonites were only one small part of a revolution in the sixteenth century that repudiated a full gamut of social institutions and established the foundations of Western soceity as we know it today. Within that larger revolution, then, we search out what one particular group of people lived and died for.

1. The meaning of holiness. The focus for Anabaptist ferment was the matter of Christlike living. The state church was, to them, a big business with ecclesiastic privileges, self-serving by-laws, moral decadence, and even unfair "union dues," all of which had little to do with unqualified obedience to Christ.

2. *An attitude toward material possessions.* The Anabaptists wanted to re-create a "colony of heaven"[3] in which (a) materialism is unchristian, (b) material goods are to be used for God's glory, (c) Christians trust in God, the Provider, (d) unchristian attitudes toward money and possessions cause the world's evils, (e) extreme economic variation—concentrated wealth or paralyzing poverty—are wrong, (f) true fellowship approaches an economic equality, and (g) the Christian community practices mutual aid, generous sharing, and cooperation.

3. *Separation from the world.* Faith, repentance, conformity to Scriptures, witnessing, living in peace with all people—such were the articles of the Anabaptists' faith. But one article, listed in the 1527 Schleitheim Confession, fixed itself for centuries into the philosophy and deeds of the Mennonites—separation from the world. They believed that God, in calling them into a binding relationship with each other, had called them out from the world, and even from fellowship with papal and Reformed church services, from patronizing drinking houses, and from participating in civic matters.[4]

Persecution helped to establish this article of faith. Mennonites, in hiding, could hardly help but see their identity as different from that of their pursuers. Later in the seventeenth and eighteenth centuries, when guild rulings excluded Mennonites from participation in the professional or craft affiliations, separation as a doctrine gradually evolved into aloofness as a business reflex.

4. *Union with the church of Christ.* According to historian J. C. Wenger, "salvation for the Anabaptists was not a private ticket to heaven."[5] Rather, it meant that a person, delivered from sin, would then unite with the

body of believers to live out in words and actions the will of Christ. This body was expected to exercise strict discipline internally as well as to give witness externally.

5. *Service.* To do God's will required giving the cup of cold water and going the second mile. One of the familiar names in Mennonite history is Dirk Willems who in 1569 turned back to rescue a pursuing officer who had broken through the ice. Dirk was then recaptured and burned at the stake.

6. *Simplicity.* As early as 1525 it was said of the Swiss Brethren, "They shun costly clothing, they shun expensive food and drink, clothe themselves with course cloth, cover their heads with broad felt hats. Their entire manner of life is completely humble."[6] The simple way of life in speech, workmanship, and conduct persisted long enough to gain for Mennonites and Amish the label "the plain people."

There are other legacies to the Anabaptist tradition: the nonswearing of oaths, the refusal to bear arms, an insistence upon separation of church and state, adult baptism, the evangelical witness, the hesitancy to establish binding relations with nonbelievers.

C. The Later Mennonite Experience

Our attention, in this section, is fixed upon the issues of business and labor after the first, intense years of this new movement.

1. *The discouragement of profit-making.* Business as an activity of buying and selling for profit was long frowned upon by Christians as not worthy of a Christlike life, writes J. Winfield Fretz.[7] This disapproval continued long after the Reformation, he notes. "Mennonites,

longer than any other religious group, forbade their members to engage in profit-making businesses."

(An exception "proved" the misgiving. Those Mennonites who, in the seventeenth and eighteenth centuries, settled into the more tolerant cities of Holland and North Germany, and there made fortunes in shipping, banking, and merchandising, soon adopted a lifestyle quite alien to that of the peasants of South Germany, Switzerland, and elsewhere. Most Mennonites chose this latter way.)

2. *The focus on farm vocations.* When Menno Simons wrote in 1544, "Rent a farm, milk cows, learn a trade if possible, do manual labor as did Paul, and all that which you then fall short of will doubtlessly be given and provided you by pious brethren,"[8] hardly could he have imagined the future of farming for Mennonites. They eventually gained an international reputation for agriculture, prompting Catherine II, empress of Russia, personally to invite German Mennonites in 1786 to emigrate to the Ukraine to develop her recently acquired lands. While the rural vocations may have assured a separation from the world and a simple lifestyle, it led to a closed subculture, a demise of evangelical zeal, and a dissipation of prophetic utterance.

3. *A respect for hard work.* The Book of Proverbs has set quite well among Mennonites; diligence became somewhat sanctified. One scholar of the eighteenth century wrote, "In no court records are there complaints or charges of the authorities or other people against the Mennonites on the point of laziness or shiftlessness, but on the contrary, they are always praised as quiet and industrious people."[9]

4. An insistence upon honesty. Truth-telling in 1535 meant giving an honest accounting of faith in the lordship of Christ. Truth-telling meant, for thousands, a cruel martyrdom. Truth-telling became a habit, a manner of speech, a code of conduct. If one lived by the code, "Let your yea be yea, and your nay be nay," one did not need a Bible to swear on. Daily living could also dare to be transparent: a bushel was measured full and running over; a day's work was defined by either the termination of the day or the completion of the work, whichever was longer; "a man's word was as good as his bond."

D. Mennonites Today

The twentieth century has done so much to Mennonites—modernized them, urbanized them, professionalized them, secularized them, homogenized them into the big mix. Can the old fathers and the old farmers speak today without sounding a little naive?

Kermit Eby, a member of the Church of the Brethren, who spent his adult years in the business, political, educational, and religious world of Chicago, asked near the close of his life, "How can we give meaning to the Judeo-Christian ethic which developed in a rather simple face-to-face village society, and transplant this ethic to a world in which issues become increasingly complex, and decision many steps removed from the individual?"[10]

A starting point in wrestling with Eby's question in history might be, What can we learn from the past that can be applied today?

Questions for Discussion

1. If you in your firm were asked to do research for a

powerful chemical to assure population control would you participate? If your job demanded building components for lethal weapons which eventually went to the Defense Department, could you participate?

2. "No servant can be the slave of two masters." In your various occupations, where have you had to decide which master you would serve?

3. One hundred years ago, God was trying to work out His purpose in your community. Can you now identify decisions that fulfilled God's purposes? that fought God's purposes?

4. Can a Christian, who wants to keep the kingdom of God first, survive when the workday is very long and the working conditions unpleasant?

5. Identify one kind of decision you must make this week that is quite unlike any decisions Christ had to make. What are some decisions similar to those Christ faced?

6. When, during the past week, did you petition for justice benefiting yourself? benefiting another person?

7. What would be the effect upon the businesses represented in your congregation if they adhered to a strict separation from the way the world does things?

8. Do you think business persons could succeed economically if they followed minutely the principles of early Anabaptist-Mennonite living?

9. Can you identify other principles for ethical business and labor practices that emerge from other particular religious heritages? (For example, the Seventh-day Adventists have operated many excellent hospitals worldwide. What principles have enriched their sense of mission?)

An Activity

If your congregation is in the Mennonite-Anabaptist tradition, where does it stand in matters related to business and labor? Each class member should browse in the book *Anabaptists Four Centuries Later*, by Howard Kauffman and Leland Harder (Herald Press, 1975). Make an intelligent guess on how your own congregation would compare with the Kauffman-Harder profiles. Numbers indicate the page on which the following charts can be found:

1. Percentage Distribution of Church Members by Sex and Occupation, 60.
2. Percentage Distribution of Church Members by Denomination and Household Income, 62.
3. Measures of Associationalism, 67.
4. Anabaptism Scale Scores, 116 (see definitions, 115).
5. Percentage Distribution of Responses on Moral Issues, 123.
6. Measures of Pacifism, 133.
7. Measures of Welfare Attitudes, 142.
8. Attitudes Toward Labor Unions, 147.
9. Per Member Giving for U.S., Canadian, and Participating Churches in 1971, 234.
10. Stewardship Attitudes, 236.
11. Rural-Urban Residence by Denominations, 284.

Discuss your findings.

References for Further Study

A. From the Bible

Matthew 5, 6, 7 (Christ's standard for ethical living).

B. From church periodicals

Rudy Dyck, "Work the Jesus Way," *Mennonite*

Brethren Herald, February 20, 1976.

Elmer A. Martens, "Reflections on the biblical view of the soil," *The Mennonite,* August 17, 1976; *Gospel Herald,* July 27, 1976.

C. From religious textbooks

Walter Klaassen, *Anabaptism: Neither Catholic nor Protestant* (Conrad Press, 1973).

John L. Ruth, *Conrad Grebel, Son of Zurich* (Herald Press, 1975).

D. From books about ethics

William Stringfellow, *An Ethic for Christians and Other Aliens in a Strange Land* (Word Books, 1973).

E. Other sources

Check your local or church library for reference works such as an encyclopedia (e.g., *The Mennonite Encyclopedia).* Browse through the index for words such as "business," "occupations," "capitalism," "work ethic," "labor," and "money."

CHAPTER THREE

The Uses and Abuses of Power

Purposes

A. To identify expressions of personal power.
B. To examine the nature of "the powers that be."
C. To become aware how business, by its nature, relates to power.
D. To understand what Jesus did with power.

Essay

"Don't throw your weight around," we scold the bully as he abuses power for personal advantage. Our resentment of bully-activity leads us to repudiate all forms of power. But power is not that easily disposed of.

Jesus the Servant-King was brought before Pilate, the powerful governor of Judea who was irritated by this disturber of civil tranquility. He ordered that his soldiers whip Jesus and that an object lesson be presented for this pretender. Yet, even after a crown was placed on His head and a robe draped on His beaten shoulders, Jesus still did not seem to comprehend the situation. "You know," Pilate told Him, "that I have authority to release you, and I have authority to crucify you."

But Jesus was aware of other forms of power about which Pilate knew little. Jesus answered, "You would have not authority at all over me, if it had not been granted you" (John 19:11). In essence, Jesus is saying that Pilate is unaware of the complexity of power and of varieties of power available. Pilate, John says, was afraid.

Both of these men, as it turns out, had great power. But what kind of power and how was it used? These questions invite a more careful study of the difference between using and abusing power. Let us examine both personal power and impersonal "powers that be."

A. Expressions of Personal Power

"What a powerful person!" is in itself an ambiguous statement, for it may refer to personal charisma or possibly to administrative clout.

There is such a thing as birth power. Not all people are created with equal power. One has muscular strength, the next is physically handicapped. One is an intellectual genius, the next a slow learner. One talent, two talents, five talents—power is a natural gift, given at birth.

Experience may give power. Two sisters or brothers endowed with similar birth power may by age 30 differ immensely from each other because of differing experiences. One opportunity, however small, later turns into a power lever.

Being powerful sometimes means being at the right place at the right time. A farmer, who in 1950 struggled to make a living off 100 acres which were located seven miles from the city, may awaken in 1977 to discover that the acreage, now in the city, is worth a million. Time and place have altered the person's power.

One can get power by being given power. Children at play stand by the sidewalks and hold up their hands like policemen, signaling the cars to stop. Their motions are disregarded; the state has not given them authority.

These examples show that personal power takes many forms: attributes given at birth, the advantage of experience, the endowment bestowed by position, the authority delegated from a higher power. More examples and expressions of personal power may be identified.

B. The "Powers That Be"

Scriptures refer to "principalities and powers" as well as to "thrones and dominions." These terms are sometimes associated with cosmological references to angels, elements, heights, and depths. What are these powers? Whom do they represent?

An excellent study source in answering those questions is Hendrik Berkhof's *Christ and the Powers* (Herald Press, 1962). While these references to "the powers" have in the past been linked with supernatural forces, modern biblical scholarship emphasizes an earth base which we might equate with political, sociological, economic, or other "forces." One theologian suggests that we think of "structures that make things happen."[1]

In some cases this "power structure" may be a large network or system. At other times, it may be a person (a sheriff, for example). Then again, it may be an abstract concept such as communism or Madison Avenue.

These structures guide the activities on earth and provide patterns for thought and behavior. Without such structures, the three billion earth people would quickly fall into erratic confusion, like a flock of frightened chickens.

C. Business and Power

If, for some curious reason, somebody took a "power audit" of a group of people—the members of your congregation, let us say—the results would likely reveal that:

1. Every person has at least some power.
2. All people differ in their power potential, just as they differ in many other ways.
3. Those persons active in business would be considered rather powerful.

Business and personal power are related. This is not to say that *all* business people have strong personalities. Nor does it indicate that a person who earns $50,000 yearly can't possibly be a weakling. But in general, the force which enervates business attracts people with power potential, and excludes the powerless. Persons in business are likely to enjoy high-energy activities, likely to be located in at least two or three positions of important decision-making, and are likely to have authority that makes what they do "stick."

Further, business and economic issues are an integral part of "the powers that be." We do not appreciate fully enough the power of economic endeavor in shaping not only our communities but the world. The life and death of one person, the rise and fall of a nation, may be brought about primarily by economic factors. Certainly in the 1970s, the worldwide structures were immediately affected by oil and natural gas.

When we realize that we are numbered with the

powerful, and are, in fact, a part of "the powers that be," we say to Jesus Christ, "Say the word. Heal our servants. Heal us." Jesus, who admired the powerful centurion's faith, can help us. (See Luke 7:1-10.)

D. Jesus, a Peculiar Model

Jesus' life gives to us a definite standard regarding both personal power and our relation to "the powers."

No one on earth knew better than did the devil that Jesus, God's own Son, carried full credentials for being powerful. "The divine nature was his from the first" (Philippians 2:6). So when the devil tried to make an offer that Jesus couldn't refuse, the deal had to do with an abuse of power. The sly devil proposed, "All these [kingdoms of the world in all their glory] . . . I will give you, if you will only fall down and do me homage" (Matthew 4:9).

But Jesus "did not think to snatch at equality with God," explains the Apostle Paul. He "made himself nothing, assuming the nature of a slave. . . . He humbled himself, and in obedience accepted even death" (Philippians 2:6-8).

On other occasions (such as in the Garden of Gethsemane) Jesus rejected the prospect of manipulative force.

Did this Jesus, who became a slave, have any character left? Was He a faceless, characterless, passive nobody? C. Norman Kraus explains that Jesus' total surrender to God's authority paradoxically gave Him power. God sent it to Him, so that He could do God's work of casting out demonic forces. Instead of becoming earth's exclusive "wonder boy," Jesus passed this same power to His followers so that they too could fight the devils. When Jesus used power, He didn't have an eye on His own advancement, but on the establishment of the kingdom of God.[2]

Little surprise, then, that when His disciples jealously bickered about their comparative status, Jesus said, "In the world, kings lord it over their subjects; and those in authority are called their country's 'Benefactors.' Not so with you: on the contrary, the highest among you must bear himself like the youngest, the chief of you like a servant" (Luke 22:25-27).

Christ recognized the powers of the earth and knew that man, in his humanity, was subject to them. Writes John Howard Yoder, "Man's subordination to these Powers is what makes him human, for if they did not exist there would be no history nor society nor humanity. If then God is going to save man in his humanity, the Powers cannot simply be destroyed or set aside or ignored. Their sovereignty must be broken."[3]

That Jesus accomplished through His death. Berkhof says, "By the cross Christ abolished the slavery which lay over our existence. . . . On the cross he 'disarmed' the Powers, 'made a public example of them and thereby triumphed over them.' "[4]

Jesus' attitude toward power contains several parts:

1. Jesus recognized the power of God.
2. He rejected the temptation to accumulate power for selfish interests.
3. When power was given to Him, He transformed it and channeled it to people in need.
4. He shared power with others, stipulating their same transforming and channeling of power.

5. He described this role as being that of a servant rather than lord, king, benefactor, philanthropist, or do-gooder.

6. With His death, Christ "disarmed" the powers and called us to a "higher destiny."[5]

E. The Jesus Way in Business and Labor

How might Jesus be a model for business managers and laborers? Here are several propositions offered by Christian business people.

1. *Seek first the kingdom of God.* If that search is genuine, then the quest for earthly power cannot be first, nor second, nor third.

2. *In serving others, we gain power.* Wesley Michaelson, an aid to Senator Mark Hatfield, has written, "If we accept Christ's principles as true, then real power and leadership do not come through position, prestige, or how well one's name is known, but through the washing of another's feet. In any context—corporate, personal, whatever—serving is where power comes from."[6]

3. *Power should be given or withheld purposefully and unselfishly.* A business or labor executive, once in control of power, can keep it close and thus deprive others of power, or like Jesus, can give the power away.

4. *Power should be harnessed into social justice.* Samuel Southard, a business consultant, has warned that the executive who grabs for power and keeps it for himself is in trouble, for power alone can tempt the executive to become authoritarian, judgmental, a rigid rule setter, greedy, and covetous. On the other hand, if the executive is self-righteous with personal concern, he can become an impulsive sentimentalist and do-gooder, lacking backbone, avoiding difficult situations.

The ethical executive, says Southard, must transform power by temperance, and he must transform personal concern by prudence. Only then can he have the precision, balance, and force to channel the power to create social justice in the corporation or organization.[7]

5. *Power should be used to fight demonic forces.* Just as Christ called upon God's power to cast out the forces of evil, so people in business and labor should, as stewards of power, exert a force against any demonic initiative that fights the purpose of God or that destroys people.

Of these several propositions, the most important is the first one. Jesus calls the manager and the laborer into His kingdom; the economic structures and forces and procedures and allegiances and codes—all of these earthly powers become secondary to the claims of God's kingdom. Whatever measure of earthly power is given to us, is to be used to build the kingdom of God.

A total obedience to God, and a dependence upon His power, may cause quite a stir within our work-a-day lives. We may have to take some unpopular stances, we may have to work harder, we may have to quit a job. But the kingdom is first.

Questions for Discussion

1. If your administrator corrects your work rather abrasively, how do you respond to his power? If you are an adminstrator, have you ever misused your power?

2. What kinds of personal power are desirable for an Avon representative? A kindergarten teacher? a John Deere dealer? a stock consultant? a housing contractor?

3. Do you feel uneasy around people in your congrega-

tion who are more talented in certain areas than you are?

4. Who are some of the people who have control over your job description? your salary?

5. Identify some of the "powers that be" which play an important part in your community.

6. How does economic power affect your local zoning commission? the high school orchestra? the crime rate? medical service? condition of dwellings?

7. Was Jesus a powerful person? Explain.

8. Share with class members a particular power you have. Tell how it might be channeled for God. Ask members to pray for your faithfulness in using this power for God's purposes.

9. What about the member of your class or congregation who feels powerless? (Or are no such persons around you?) What is an appropriate response to a person who suffers from an inferiority complex, from an unfulfilling role, from unsatisfactory employment?

An Activity

Game theory has been used widely to analyze real-life situations. Many games contain the dynamics of power brokerage. During the next week, each member should participate in one game (a table game, an athletic game, etc.) and without revealing the assignment to other participants, watch for evidence of:

1. Power exerted through physical strength.
2. Power exerted through memory.
3. Power exerted through one's secret knowledge.
4. Power exerted through collusion (working secretly with a partner).
5. Power exerted through trickery.

6. Power exerted through coercion.

At the next class session, report the findings. How did you react to the power-brokerage? Were you powerful or powerless?

References for Further Study

A. From the Bible

James 2, 4, 5 (teachings about abuse of power).

B. From church periodicals

Larry Kehler, "Parable of the Overgifted," *The Mennonite*, August 3, 1976.

"North American Food Power," (an interview with Leonard Siemens) in *Mennonite Brethren Herald*, August 6, 1976, and in *Gospel Herald*, October 12, 1976.

John H. Redekop, "Mennonite Millionaires," *Mennonite Brethren Herald*, March 19, 1976.

C. From religious textbooks

Hendrik Berkhof, *Christ and the Powers* (Herald Press, 1962).

John Howard Yoder, *The Politics of Jesus* (Eerdmans, 1972).

D. From books about ethics

Samuel Southard, *Ethics for Executives* (Thomas Nelson, 1975).

E. Other sources

Three magazines have contributed many fine articles about the business ethics question: *Atlantic*, *Harpers*, and *Saturday Review*.

CHAPTER FOUR

Labor Relations

Purposes

A. To examine our stereotypes of the so-called antagonists in labor relations—: "the manager" and "the laborer."

B. To review the development of both organized labor and organized management.

C. To summarize attitudes of church people toward management labor relations.

D. To suggest a principle for effective labor relations.

Essay

This year I attended a business banquet. The dinner speaker, with confident voice and expansive gestures, told the audience, "Unless you're sophisticated enough to know how it works, you could be unsophisticated enough to have to work for somebody else."[1]

In these few words he stereotyped two camps. Management—the sophisticated ones. Labor—the unsophisticated ones. The banqueters were nearly all managers, but I, somewhat unlabeled, listened to their chuckles and reflected upon what a sociologist had earlier told me: "There is no other issue that so divides the Christian business community as does the labor/management tension."[2]

A. Who Is "the Manager?"

The stereotyped manager is the owner, the employer, the director, the foreman, whoever qualifies as being "the boss." Managers supposedly get their exalted positions through luck or through pluck, and once they've "made it," they wear white shirts, work easy hours, get high salaries, but are prone to heart attacks, or at least ulcers.

He—and occasionally she—is supposed to be a futures thinker, standard-setter, initiator of action, risk-taker, personnel manager, operations controller, communicator, criticism receiver.

The stereotype might be extended. It is not a myth, however, that the manager interacts with other managers, uses the accessories that make corporate action efficient, and often makes decisions in an atmosphere of carpets, curtains, and coffee tables. Managers can become estranged from labor.

Incidentally, the manager is a person—fragile and breakable. The farther to fall, the more pieces to break into. There is a vulnerability in leadership that few outsiders can identify with. Non-managers may never know the anxiety, the sense of inadequacy, the demands of crucial decisions that managers face constantly. Maybe that is why people in our culture get some delight in seeing a person of high position, influence, and power tumble to destruction.

B. Who Is "the Laborer?"

Laborers can be stereotyped too. They wear blue collars and hard hats, have red necks, and sometimes type 70 words per minute. They do not show sufficient intelligence, skill, or initiative to be managers, loaf too much, take orders reluctantly, and run to the parking lot at quitting time to get ahead of the traffic. Laborers hurry to the bank drive-up teller on Friday nights, and according to the exhaustive study, "Work in America," would change jobs if given the right opportunity.

To an outsider, it may seem that the worker never had it so good. Safety standards are higher, noise levels are lower. There's a minimum wage, a 40-hour week, and retirement benefits. And yet, the laborer is depressed. What is wrong?

I asked a group of workers during an industrial seminar to write down their complaints. Their listing is included here, not because it is representative of grievances, but because it shows the immediacy of the worker's travail.

1. We need a friendlier atmosphere where "good morning" and "how are you?" are our daily bread.
2. I've a dozen bosses. To whom am I *really* responsible?
3. What's my job, and the next guy's job? We get into each other's territories.
4. Rules and regulations, sure. But why are the rules stretched for some people, and not for others?
5. I wish I could erase the feeling that I am a flunky, not qualified to do other than menial tasks.
6. I've been around long. To this day I haven't received a genuine compliment for my work.
7. The big shots don't consider me to be a human being—a person important enough to be informed of decisions and changes.

8. Gossip hurts us. We cut each other up.
9. I am bored. I see no purpose in doing my job well. And so I watch the clock.

After reading through these profiles of the manager and the laborer one is aware that they are a mixture of fact and fiction. By thinking of familiar persons who do not fit these stereotypes we can try to correct our own impressions of these two "antagonists."

C. Organized Labor

A labor union is an association of workers yoked together for a power advantage.

Labor unions are as old as Western civilization,[3] reaching back to medieval *frith guilds* and *craft guilds*. When the industrial revolution brought with it the factory system, many worker grievances about the sweatshops and child labor and legal slavery gave such an impetus to unionism that by 1886 the Knights of Columbus—a union of skilled and unskilled, manual, clerical, and professional workers—numbered 1,000,000. Today, more than one in five in the United States belongs to a union.[4] Unionism is big business.

The history of union growth reads roughly. Few shops became unionized prior to 1930 without a fierce fight. On the one side were union terrorists like the Molly Maguires who fought the Pennsylvania anthracite coal magnates in 1877 and the "Wobblies" who in the early part of this century tried to overthrow capitalism through violence. On the other side of the battle lines were the arsenals of weapons, the military, dogs, police, and national guardsmen protecting management.

Unions have differed so widely it is hard to make safe

generalizations about all unions. Usually, one may venture to say, unions want:

1. Collective bargaining for wages, working conditions, and benefits.
2. Legal defense and redress for grievances.
3. A political lobby or more direct political power.
4. And, in some cases, representation on managements' control boards.

Because unionism and politics are related, the United States and Canadian governments have waffled on unionism. During conservative eras, governments fight unions. During liberal eras, governments encourage unions. For example, in the United States, Democratic pressures brought about the pro-labor National Labor Relations Act of 1935 while Republican pressures checked labor in the Taft-Hartley Act of 1947.

D. Organized Management

The banding together of people in management is as old and as pervasive, but strangely not as controversial, as labor unionism. The craft guilds of the middle ages were no more unique than the merchant guilds which tried to protect monopoly operations.

In the nineteenth and twentieth centuries, organized management has taken many forms: professional associations, conventions, trade publications, syndicates, chains, mergers and amalgamations, subsidiary relationships, and of course, the corporation entity itself.

Union workers have their social centers; managers are admitted to Rotary Club. Unions vote in blocks; organized management pays election bills (sometimes illegally). Union chiefs line their pockets with hundreds of thousands of dollars; management salaries are not lower. The unions are linked to the underworld; management has recently been charged with collusion with foreign governments. The size of union membership is dangerously huge; but American Telephone and Telegraph, on the other hand, absorbed in 1974 almost 20 percent of the capital that all United States corporations raised from outside sources.

I myself was briefly associated with one such management organization, The New York State Newspaper Publishers Association. The motives were clear: fraternization on the one hand, and self-serving coercion on the other—in Albany, in Washington, in courtrooms, at picket lines. It was impossible for me to escape the comparison of NYSNPA with the craft unions serving the newspaper back shop.

E. Attitudes Toward Labor and Management

Only an anarchist would insist that managers are unnecessary. But are unions necessary? I happened to scribble the first draft of this very paragraph in the hospital. My roommate, "Old Man Wyatt," struggled for his breath after having worked in the coal mines. Before the second draft of this paragraph was written, Old Man Wyatt had died. Black lung disease. The workers' situation all of a sudden became personal and believable for me. Old Man Wyatt, and now his widow, needed a union.

On the other hand, both labor and management can be accused of increased militancy, lying, and deception, crippling strikes, disrespect for signed contracts and the law of the land, decreased concern about public welfare, unreasonable salary offers and demands, collusion with undesirable organizations, and a general dissipation of our work ethic.[5]

Can we find help for shaping our attitudes toward labor and management from the experience of the Christian church? The Christian church accepted the tenets of capitalism uncritically at first.[6] It is hard to believe that church people did not object to Adam Smith in 1748 when he wrote, "Wages paid . . . must be such as may enable them . . . to continue the race of journeymen and servants . . . to subsist and perpetuate their race, without either increase or diminution."[7]

It was not the Protestants but the Catholic hierarchy which was the first in the eighteenth and nineteenth centuries to address the welfare of the masses. Visionaries such as Cardinal Nicholas Wiseman in 1850 argued that the mission of the church was not in the splendor of Westminster Abbey but in the lanes and courts and alleys and slums. In 1891, a papal encyclical suggested standards for right relations between workers and employers.

Meanwhile, Protestants sided with management. Those who first worked for the cause of the laborer were extremists—first socialists and later the advocates of the social gospel. Not until 1946 could Protestants join Catholics and Jews in a statement on economic justice.

Now the scene has changed considerably. John Kenneth Galbraith says, "Until about thirty years ago the primary object of economic criticism in the United States was the labor union; it resisted innovation, raised costs, subjected the community to the inconvenience of strikes, and was in highly unauthorized possession of an essentially public power. . . . But, overwhelmingly, the modern focus of critical discussion is on the great corporation."[8]

This shift is reflected, for instance, in the 1967 declaration by the Commission on Church and Economic Life of the National Council of Churches: "The right to strike is ethically defensible so long as it is essential to the achievement of justice and freedom for workers, and the only way to eliminate strikes is to develop alternate strategies for the protection of freedom and justice which render strikes unnecessary."

One might examine and learn from the experience of one of the historic peace churches, the Mennonites, in their attitudes about this topic. By eliminating exceptions to the rule, one may delineate four "eras" in Mennonite history and thought.

Era 1. The first generation of Anabaptist-Mennonites in Europe (1525-1555) taught "nothing but love, faith, and the cross. . . . They broke bread with each other. . . . They helped each other faithfully . . . lending, borrowing, giving, and taught that all things should be common, [and] called each other brothers. . . ."[9] A contemporary scholar, Walter Klaassen, says, "All Anabaptists agreed that in the kingdom of God of which they knew themselves to be citizens there could be no 'mine' and 'thine.' "[10] The forefathers discouraged the vocation of trader or merchant, but at the same time taught against any kind of coercive action.

Era 2. Because of persecution, the "colony of heaven" retreated into earthly agriculture; Mennonites became the "quiet of the land." As they adopted a lifestyle of nonconformity to the world, nonresistance, nonswearing of oaths, avoidance of secret societies, avoidance of "unequal yokes" with unbelievers, they lost touch with urban life, the industrial revolution, and organizational complexities around them. This era continued for well over three centuries.

Era 3. As union-management warfare broke out in the latter nineteenth century, Mennonites took a typically rural, conservative stance toward the labor movement. A number of conferences in the Mennonite Church drafted official actions against their members' joining unions: Franconia in 1881, Indiana-Michigan in 1891, Ontario in 1901, and Amish-Mennonite (Eastern) in 1907. The General Conference Mennonite Church opposed any type of worker violence. One might designate the close of this era to be 1941 when the Mennonite Church and the Brethren in Christ Church issued a statement that protested conflict, injustice, and retaliation both of labor groups, manufacturers, and employers associations and even agriculturists. The statement continued to prohibit union membership, although the issue was presented in the larger context of a class struggle in which labor and management were fighting for power. The Mennonite Brethren adopted the same statement, except that they permitted union membership.

Era 4. Since the 1940s, much has happened economically to Mennonites. Some who have moved into managerial positions or become entrepreneurs have taken their cues from secular management philosophy, and mouth the rhetoric of the anti-labor bias. On the other side, some Mennonites "in the shop" have sided with the motives of labor, but feel uncomfortable with some of the strategies. Meanwhile a new generation of Mennos has argued that the church is following "ideological fancies" rather than being faithful to scriptural imperatives. "I think it unfair, illogical, and ideologically biased," writes one, "for Mennonites to exhibit resistance to labor union structures while at the same time applying no sanctions and asking no questions of the capitalistic enterprise."[11] Another person questions "the inherent and structural violence and coercion that exist with other organizations, such as the doctors' and lawyers' monopoly of their respective professions. They have simply acquired more subtle ways of achieving the same ends as the labor unions."[12]

The Kauffman-Harder studies[13] document the occupational and sociological changes among Mennonites. "The more urbanized a member becomes, the more open he becomes to participation in the political process, the more education he has, and the higher he has risen in the socioeconomic ladder, the less he adheres to the official (anti-labor union) position."

F. A Principle for Labor-Management Relations

It is impossible in any document, much less this short study guide, to deliver a formula to solve all labor-management questions. But I should like to close this essay with the mere suggestion of a principle for decision making.

When one looks closely at God's plan for His people, the design features uncompromised wholeness. For the Christian community there can be no higher standard for ethical living than the principle of spiritual, social, economic, physical wholeness—for oneself and for others.

I have identified the principle; the church community should now seek to apply the principle in management and labor issues. One might wish to refer again to lesson one that dealt with the integrity (wholeness) of the Christian fellowship; to lesson two that dealt with the inclusiveness (wholeness) of the purpose of God in history and the expressions of holy (wholeness) living in the experience of the Christian church; to lesson three to Jesus' quest for sanity (wholeness) in regard to the use of power; and later to lesson five which will deal with a harmony (wholeness) between our jobs and our service to God.

John Redekop, whom we have quoted several times in these lessons, apparently had in mind the principle suggested here when, in a 1975 lecture to medical practitioners he said, "What could be more fitting than to have that arm of the church which is specifically committed to bring wholeness to the individual man's body, mind, and soul also zero in on the need to replace hatred with wholeness in employer-employee affairs."[14]

The questions that follow will further guide your inquiry into the meaning of wholeness in labor-management relations.

Questions for Discussion

1. When you hear that a person was fired for asking—too loudly—for a retirement policy, with whom do you identify? the employer? or the laborer?

2. Let business persons describe a typical week's schedule with its responsibilities, associations, and meetings that make them "lose track" of the employees. Discuss how the manager might resist the pressure to be sealed off from other workers.

3. Let laborers describe how they can make the isola-

tion between manager and laborer worse through gossip, ill will, the placing of blame, refusal to associate, and the like.

4. Review the profiles of managers and laborers at the beginning of the essay. Who are people you know who do not fit these characteristics?

5. Why do 70 percent of workers want to change jobs? Is that figure to be expected, or does it indicate a malady in our system of work?

6. In your professional associations, how do you as a Christian handle the following: militancy? coercion? absenteeism from home? double scheduling with church functions? the cocktail mentality? dirty language? political activity?

7. At your place of work, does a healthy relationship exist between labor and management? What has been one of your more satisfying conversations with one of your managers? one of your laborers?

8. In which of the four Mennonite eras could you most comfortably live?

9. How could your church improve its approach to labor-management issues?

An Activity

Let each member make an "audit" of a local business' labor-management policies. Explain your purpose to the management (you might even offer *Ethics in Business and Labor* to the manager and to the director of personnel). Obtain a copy of the policies. Then, perhaps over coffee, gather information about the unwritten policies as well as the performance of management and laborers in carrying out the policies. Does the business have good policies? Are the policies well stated and understood by everyone? Are the people able to carry out the policies? After studying the data, invite the manager and an employee to come to class for a discussion with you about the project, your responses, and their responses to you.

References for Further Study

A. From the Bible

Colossians 2:6-15 and 3:1—4:6 (standards for social justice).

B. From church periodicals

Wally Kroeker, "What City Cousins Should Know About Farming," *Gospel Herald,* July 27, 1967; *The Mennonite,* August 17, 1976.

John H. Redekop, "Do Christian Workmen Need to Join the Fight?" *Mennonite Brethren Herald,* February 20, 1976, and "Another Way for Christian Workmen," March 5, 1976.

C. From religious textbooks

John H. Redekop, *Labor Problems in Christian Perspective* (Eerdmans, 1972).

D. From books about ethics

William A. Spurrier, *Ethics and Business* (Charles Scribner's Sons, 1962). Note especially chapters 6 and 7.

E. Other sources

The Youth-Adult Uniform Lessons for October 3—November 28, 1976, published by the Mennonite Publishing House and Faith and Life Press, deal with reconciliation.

CHAPTER FIVE

Christian Vocation: Job and Service

Purposes

A. To expose our tendency to separate our jobs from our service to God.

B. To give to the definition of Christian vocation the wholeness it deserves.

C. To inquire of ways that servanthood, in a Christian community, can become a crucial dynamic in business activities.

Essay

When the party companions asked about her grown children, Mrs. Miller brightened into a glow: "Why Tom's in real estate—you surely see his signs all over town. Chet—you know him—his law office up in Stanfordville is busier all the time. Mary's own children are now in school, so she's employed part time in Joe Kepler's store. And Pete, of course, is in the ministry."

Mrs. Miller talks just like the rest of us do. We're "in business," "in ceramics," "in teaching," "in service." We make neat little compartments, and those we divide into religious and secular categories. We've all heard a statement like this: "Dorothy and I hope to put another good five years into the business, get things established, then we'd like to give a couple of years to Voluntary Service."

Why do we follow this unconscious tendency to separate those vocations which belong to the Lord from those quite removed from "the cloth"? Why do the categories of vocation and occupation force us into categorical thinking?

A. Categorical Thinking

Putting up a fence between Christian service and "my regular job" is not a recently acquired habit. A dichotomy called dual ethics reaches far back into Christian history. Already in the time of Constantine, people felt a dilemma between a Christian ethic and a sense of public responsibility. Later, during the Middle Ages, it was only a minority of the saints "with extraordinary spiritual health who were able and were expected to maintain the strenuous ethic of love, nonresistance, and brotherhood." Others were resigned to a lesser standard. There were two classes of Christian vocation: on the higher level, the priests, monks, and nuns "provided a vicarious substitute for the substandard Christianity of the worldly Christians of the lower level."[1]

Such categories, once established, don't change easily. St. Thomas Aquinas, and later Luther and other Reformers, while finding new power in the supernatural way of the cross, could not be assured that this new way provided directions for the ordinary Christian in ordinary jobs.

Calvin, then, developed his doctrine of "sphere sovereignty" that allowed church, state, family, school, occupational agencies, and the like, each to serve God, but each according to its own laws. While Calvinists believed in a kingly God who was strict enough to reign supremely over all these spheres, yet each sphere tended to usurp a sovereignty of its own, with its own authorities, privileges, strategies, and even ethics.

While we might not use the words "sphere sovereignty," our ways of thinking about job and service come very close to dualism. In Voluntary Service one is a servant of the Lord; in current vocation, one is his own boss. In any given week, a person may participate in the most contradictory of activities, some of which we call "sacred" and others "secular." The locations, the kinds of associates, the types of humor, the selections of food and drink, the procedures for making decisions, the accepted attire, and even the assumptions about what is right and wrong trap us in weird incongruities. Imagine, for example, the person who has come from the combative, greedy, individualistic, high-pressured job, singing softly in church, "peace, perfect peace."

In the same way that the breakdown between the sacred and secular can be associated with forces in historical theology, so the alienation between occupations can be linked with forces in economics. The exclusiveness among workmen, established by the guilds in the Middle Ages, provided a perfect fit for the specialization of the Industrial Revolution. In our technological Western world, we have not only seen from afar the exclusive power of trade and professional organizations, but we have been asked to give loyalty to our respective guilds or unions or associations. Our jobs claim the best hours of the day and the greater part of our energies. We agree to respect the employer, cooperate with fellow employees, obey codes of conduct, and follow accepted procedures. Such claims may be quite different from those of one's own household. A 40-year-old personnel manager recently admitted, "I have a car, so I could buzz home from work at five o'clock. But I walk. And slowly at that. I must have time to leave the work world and get ready to enter my family world."

The casual comment, "Don't ask me; I only work here," is a symbol of the categorical thinking and the compartmentalization of our lives.

B. One Sovereign, One Service

For the Christian, there is only one service, and that is offered to the one Sovereign. Although the Apostle Paul was a maker of tents, he introduced himself as "servant of Christ Jesus, apostle by God's call, set apart for the service of the Gospel" (Romans 1:1).

The Christian theologian Dietrich Bonhoeffer explained the nature of our single, holistic obligation with these words:

> The question of good embraces man with his motives and purposes . . . it embraces reality as a whole, as it is held in being by God. The divine words, "Behold it was very good" (Gen. 1:31) refer to the whole of creation. The good demands the whole, not only the whole of man's outlook but his whole work, the whole man, together with the fellowmen who are given to him. . . . Man is an indivisible whole, not only as an individual in his person and work but also as a member of the community of men and creatures. . . . This indivisible whole, reality which is founded on God and ap-

> prehended in Him, is what the question of good has in view. With respect to its origin this indivisible whole is called "creation." With respect to its goal it is called the "kingdom of God." Both of these are equally remote from us and equally close to us, for God's creation and God's kingdom are present with us solely in God's self-revelation in Jesus Christ.[2]

For Bonhoeffer, God is the Creator, the Definer of the good, the Maker of reality, the Head of the divine kingdom. All of our work and each of our obligations are subjected to the claims of God's creation and God's kingdom. To fulfill those obligations, we become servants of Christ.

The wholeness that results from service to Christ is built up through personal integrity and through communal fellowship. For an example of the wholeness of personal integrity, consider the testimony of the Quaker merchant, John Woolman:[3]

> My mind, through the power of truth, was in a good degree weaned from the desire of outward greatness, and I was learning to be content with real conveniences, that were not costly, so that a way of life free from much entanglement appeared best for me, though the income might be small. I have several offers of business that appeared profitable, but I did not see my way clear to accept of them, believing they would be attended with more outward care and cumber than was required of me to engage in. I saw that an humble man, with the blessing of the Lord, might live on a little, and that where the heart was set on greatness, success in business did not satisfy the craving; but that commonly with an increase of wealth the desire of wealth increased. There was a care on my mind so to pass my time that nothing might hinder me from the most steady attention to the voice of the true Shepherd.

Wholeness is built up also through communal fellowship. The Apostle Paul recognized the diversity in the Christian fellowship when he wrote, "For Christ is like a single body with its many limbs and organs, which, many as they are, together make up one body (1 Corinthians 12:12). We Christians have much to learn in fulfilling *together* our service to Christ. One consultant for these lessons wrote, "How about the real-estate agent in the church sharing information with the person working with poverty housing, or the personnel manager sharing with the person working with the unemployed? The person in the Chamber of Commerce could be a valuable resource to the inner-city worker who does not understand power brokerage nor the ways of holding companies which discriminate. Cooperation of Christian business people with poverty and minorities workers has not been explored."

A body in Christ, with all the saints fused into a union, comprise what Guy Hershberger called "the foundation of love for human society, for the social order, and for the nations."[4]

C. Wholeness in Christian Fellowship

For those persons praying for still more discernment in knowing how to integrate job and service, work and leisure, family relationships and business associations, vocations and avocations, here is a listing of several suggestions for your discussion. Each is stated briefly; you may elaborate upon each one.

1. Identify not only your talents, but the talents of fellow Christians. Take tests (aptitude, interest inventories) or consult with career counselors. Discuss the results.
2. Help each other find opportunities to develop talents.

Encourage additional education, give a boost to someone trying a new job.

3. Observe a sabbatical. Use it for mutual support. The one day of "rest" in seven is far more than an outdated, old-fashioned idea.

4. Learn to empathize. Put yourself into the experience of a fellow Christian until you can think and feel what that person feels. Empathy destroys our glibness, our judgmental attitudes, our easy suggestions.

5. Reject exclusive individualism. We should hear Philip Slater's warning: "Community, engagement, dependency—are suppressed in our society out of a commitment to individualism. The belief that everyone should pursue her own destiny autonomously has forced us to maintain an emotional detachment from our social and physical environment."[5]

6. Allow a cross-referencing of your roles. Instead of separating family life from vocation from leisure from church, let the informations, activities, and relationships intermix and at places fuse.

7. Confide in Christian colleagues. Let them listen, counsel, and suggest, especially when the claims of our jobs seem to pull us away from the primary loyalty to Christ.

8. Admit your business into the church fellowship. Why should sermons and songs and class discussions be so antiseptically abstract? The stuff of everyday life should not be shut out of the assembly of saints (who happen to have callouses on their hands).

9. Persist for social justice. It is natural to fight for one's own rights; it is a spiritual grace to work for the rights and the full potentials of other people, including competitors.

10. Testify about God's wholeness. Many non-Christians are repulsed by constant religious "witnessing," but a "word fitly spoken" makes a good caption for a thousand living examples of Christlike living.

And then there is the possibility that your job and your

commitment to Christ are irreconcilable. If this is true, pray for the courage to change jobs. In yet other situations, the Christian may be called upon to protest wrongdoing, and in the spirit of Christ's own ministry to cast out the demonic forces that destroy God's creation and God's kingdom.

In an era of many attractive job opportunities, each of which tries to stake out a claim on our lives, we dare not forget that we are members of one body of Christ, through which we serve the one Sovereign God. With that priority established, it's possible to put in a good day's work.

Questions for Discussion

1. Is your family a part of your service for Christ in this world? Is your service on the job more important than your service at home? How do you decide when you are giving too much time to your job and not enough to your job with spouse and children?

2. When you are introduced, what phrases do people use to identify you? Do these phrases pertain to job, a skill, a personality trait, family relationship, an achievement, your faith?

3. Do the people of your congregation hold dual expectations for the members? for men as compared with women? adults as compared with youth? for the ordained persons as compared with laity?

4. In your typical week, when and where do you feel closest to service for God? When and where do you feel farthest from service to God?

5. The Scriptures refer to a variety of gifts. What if, in a congregation, there is not a great variety? Does a con-

gregation suffer if most of the members are in the same vocation? or if most of them are related to each other?

6. Some churches have dedication ceremonies for people leaving for "Christian service." What do you think of the idea of dedication ceremonies for day laborers? homemakers? secretaries? sales representatives? business managers?

7. Are you hoping to give a period of full-time work to a church agency? If so, in which arm of the church could you give some muscle?

8. Do you observe a sabbatical? In what way is it "rest" from the six days of labor? In what way do you use the sabbath to enrich others?

9. If you were asked by God to bring an offering—the very best object you have had a part in making—what would that object be? Why do you consider this one of your best?

An Activity

During the next week, write your obituary. Put into it all that really matters. Exclude all that doesn't matter. Next class session invite a total stranger to read each of the obituaries and, if appropriate, to comment on them. Then the class may wish to carry on the discussion, particularly on how to bring one's ideals and one's performance into a harmony. It may be important to note the place of one's current job/service in that obituary.

References for Further Study

A. From the Bible

Psalm 90 (a prayer to keep it all in perspective).

B. From church periodicals

Gordon Hunsberger, "Land: For Profit or for Food?" *Gospel Herald,* July 20, 1976; *Mennonite Brethren Herald,* August 6, 1976.

Hector G. Valencia V. "The Good News and the Poor: Can Wealthy People Take the Gospel to the Poor?" *The Mennonite,* August 8, 1976.

C. From religious textbooks

Guy F. Hershberger, *The Way of the Cross in Human Relations* (Herald Press, 1958).

D. From books about ethics

Joseph W. Towle, ed., *Ethics and Standards in American Business* (Houghton Mifflin, 1964).

E. Other sources

Is this the time to examine literature from Mennonite Central Committee and various mission offices to learn of service opportunities and to apply for an assignment?

CHAPTER SIX

The Road "Less Traveled By"

Purpose

A. To focus attention upon creative thinking as one of the most important opportunities for the Christian in business and labor.
B. To stimulate creative thinking by offering examples of imaginative, yet conscientious approaches to business and labor.

Essay

For ten years a truck driver may move his 18-wheel rig across the continent, doing it well—and seldom pursue a creative thought.

For twenty years a teacher may tug her students through the grammar drills—and never gain a new insight.

For thirty years a seamstress may follow the patterns. For thirty years.

There's nothing wrong with following the pattern, in doing a task the same way a hundred times, in settling into routines. Nothing wrong, unless there's a better way.

But in our topic of ethics in business and labor, being just ordinary, doing the job today as it's been done yesterday, moving things from the "in" box to the "out" box, doing business as usual, isn't good enough. Questions of ethics in business and labor are formulated by people sensitive enough to know when a problem exists. Finding solutions to those questions of ethics calls people to reject "business as usual" and to explore new alternatives.

Wrote the poet Robert Frost,

> Two roads diverged in a wood, and I—
> I took the one less traveled by,
> And that has made all the difference.[1]

A creative person and a creative church must be willing to take some roads less traveled by as new problems demand attention. When conscientious objectors to war encountered in their Civilian Public Service assignments many inhumane conditions in mental institutions, it was a signal for creative minds to devise better alternatives to mental health care. When world food shortages finally grabbed our attention, writers such as Doris Longacre began thinking about new alternatives for our own living (and eating) habits.[2] Today, of these issues demanding a creative reply, none rivals in immediacy and consequence the question of ethical business and labor endeavors.

As Christians give creative thought to business and labor issues, they will experience mixed emotions. Certainly one of the first emotions connected with creativity is exhilaration, excitement about newness. But soon exhilaration must be replaced by courage because taking the road less traveled by isn't as easy as taking the super highway. Where does the road lead? Often into a wilderness thicket, fit only for the pioneering church community.

A. Some New Ideas

To prepare this section of the essay, I did not go to textbooks nor to national news and business publications for examples of creative thinking, but instead reflected upon the efforts of people whom I have met, whose vigorous but conscientious imaginations produced something new.

I want to make all kinds of qualifications; I shouldn't. Just keep in mind that these are experiments, some of them possibly discarded by the time you read about them. Because the ideas are more important than the identity of the originators, I prefer to protect the identity of the people.

1. To appreciate money. "God is great and God is good. And we thank Him for this food." A carpenter I know scowled one day, "We pray that prayer daily, but my children hardly know its meaning. When my income is deposited into the bank account, we don't see it as a gift from God." So he got an idea. He took his weekly check to the bank, cashed it into coins and bills, and carried it home in a bag. He gathered his family around the table. Then he opened the bag and emptied its contents onto the table and prayed, "God is great and God is good." He paused, then continued, "Mother and children, this is what God has provided. Help yourselves."

2. To select a job. Harold and Roberta explained to

their home church on a Sunday morning the method whereby they decided to accept a job in another state. "We called six Christian friends together and informed them about the job opportunity, our current employment, our interests and family plans, and asked for their advice. We accepted this new job only after we and our six counselors came to a consensus on a decision."

3. *To use teamwork.* Much has been said recently about the increased fear of failure suffered by lonely persons in an individualistic society. Instead of giving most of one's energy to the fight against failure, to competition, and individual success, couldn't business people work together? Yes. In Alberta four people (two married couples) have established a business in "community services." One person has a specialty in personnel leadership, another in Indian resources, a third in methods of social research, and a fourth in interviewing and writing. Their first contract, funded by a $100,000 grant, required the skills of all four.

4. *To tackle unpleasant tasks.* A company made up of Christians was established to work in real estate—focusing on middle- and lower-income housing. The group bought run-down houses, made only the minimal repairs to allow the tenants warm and secure shelter. (They decided not to renovate houses into higher economic levels which would "eliminate" tenants who could not afford the higher rents.) They owned as many as 40 units, and have learned many things: "This town needs low-income housing," said one of the members, "and more important, low-income housing owned by moral people. The risks and the kinds of people connected with low-income housing invite unethical slum landlords. But we

will probably get out of the business. We're not making any money. And we must absorb lots of hostility, the worst of which comes from people in the higher economic brackets who expect us to provide housing at our own continued financial loss." The company has not yet folded; I hope it doesn't.

5. *To hire "unemployables."* The front page of the newspaper said it so succinctly: Joe was in jail, arrested for assault with intent to commit rape. Days later, Joe received two messages at jail, almost simultaneously. One said, "Your employment with us is, of course, terminated; where shall we send your check?" The other, from a Christian in business, said, "We're sorry to hear of your difficulties. If you should be released on bail, come to take employment with us, and maybe together you and we can begin putting together a new start." It really happened.

6. *To consider humane issues.* The president of a financial institution was forced to excuse a vice-president who, in retaliation, urged his whole department to resign. They did. One week later, a subordinate who had resigned and had found another job, returned to apologize and to ask for reinstatement in his former job. "The rules would say absolutely no," the president said. "But I thought of what had gone through the man's mind, of his image of himself, of his wife and family. I called in the other officers and jointly we agreed (1) to give him a job, (2) to reassign him to a new department, and (3) to evaluate his status in 30 days."

7. *To draw administrative charts.* Every administrative chart I'd ever seen was shown in the vertical, with the president on top and the lowest paid hourly employees

on the bottom. Then I read the administrative chart of a church agency, depicted as a horizontal process. There's not much difference between vertical and horizontal, but somehow the word *hierarchy* fitted the vertical displays and seemed irrelevant in the horizontal one. Upon visiting this church agency, I noticed that coffee break was shared around tables, with people of varying job assignments mixing freely.

8. *To select size.* "Big projects, big organizations, big government . . . the spirit of grandiosity and ego-inflation pervades our economic life," charges Philip Slater.[3] Melvin Hershey is fighting bigness. A skilled auto mechanic who has a successful car repair shop in Pennsylvania, Hershey has deliberately (1) refused to accept a new car dealer franchise, (2) refused to go into the used car business along with the repair work, (3) taken out the gasoline pumps which distracted from his chosen work, (4) refused to hire more than three other persons so that all four could together give full time to repairing cars. When fire leveled the old building, he refused to build larger. He has decided what size his business should be, rather than letting the temptation to grow bigger enslave him.

9. *To modify salary extremes.* What happens to the relationship of people who work beside each other when their salaries are quite different—thousands of dollars a year different? An unusual model that defies the established salary schedules of a particular profession comes from an agency in the Midwest whose staff voted to "squash" salaries—that is, to reduce the upper salaries in order to raise the lower salaries. The experiment has been in operation for several years.

10. To improve staff communication. It's easy to talk or write about good staff relationships, but an agency I know was serious enough about bringing that theory into their practice that it closed shop one workday. It actually closed the doors, let the phone go unanswered, and hauled its entire staff to a Michigan conference center. There, with the help of a professional counselor, the staff listened, discussed, role-played, joked, argued, problem solved, practiced, and communed on the topic of verbal and nonverbal interaction. All of the employees were paid full salary for the privilege of learning.

11. To contribute beauty. Four entrepreneurs—an architect, an artist, a craftsman, and a realtor—are now in battle against ugly suburban rectangles and crackerboxes. "Suburbia is a crime against the spirit," is their response to the jerry-built developments now gobbling up the acreage around our cities. Their strategy of battle is to make a model development internally zoned so that much of the forty-acre area will be commonly held, and given to forests, recreation areas, and gardens. The houses will be set upon smaller lots along a curving road that yields to terrain, trees, and other aesthetic factors. "But that's just not the way we develop around here," argue the officials. The four entrepreneurs are persisting, and at last report had convinced the surveyors and the zoning commission of their plan, and were ready to let contracts for roadbuilding.

12. To involve family. Many families in business are practically foreigners to other members of their own family. Children who see their dads only at bedtime have little opportunity to learn the father model. So Fred Anderson, an Ohio merchant, has established "buddy day" with his five-year-old son. For more than a year he has given one working day per week to a companionship of son with father. Son goes to the office, the stores, everywhere that the father goes. "Sure it works," says Fred.

13. To use inheritance money. Her Illinois neighbors know that she's rich, but nobody calls her "stinkin' rich." She doesn't suffer that negative label because, in her own words, "The money I inherited is only mine to administer." Instead of investing in blue chips or growth funds, she has placed the money in the hands of neighbors, friends, and people in need, charging no more interest than that given by the local Savings and Loan Association passbook plan (currently 5 percent). Her lawyer said, "She came in here to have me write up a loan for $3,000 to someone she doesn't know . . . a student. And she insisted that there be no interest rate at all until the student, two years from now, finds work. Then the rate is to be 5 percent. After I wrote these strange terms, she said, 'And now what do I owe you for your services?' Incredible!"

14. To share ownership. Sometimes it is not easy to teach a child to use the word "ours" instead of the word "mine." Can the child be blamed however, if most objects surrounding him are owned by one person? In our own community in the past several years, there has been a lot of experimenting with group ownership of necessities and luxuries, of work and play equipment. I am aware of a group of three families who together own two cars, seven families who together own a garden tractor and composter, five families who own two horses, two families who own a garden plot, three families who own a van, and three families who own a sailboat. I have noticed a tendency for more and more persons in business to share ownership rather than to "go it alone."

This listing of ideas is not complete. You may be able to add to the list. Do you know of creative ideas in—

sharing profits?
employee ownership?
elimination of discrimination?
avoidance of coercion?
refusal to exploit?
commitment to conserve natural resources?
elimination of pollution?
encouraging problem solving?
improving quality beyond the "accepted standard"?
accepting the counsel of the church?
taking a humane interest in persons?
fighting unethical practices?
decreasing the complexity, clutter, and tension of life?
building a business while strengthening the family?
integrating job and service to God?

B. Creativity Stimulates Creativity

People are like pumps that need priming. Once they are fed creative ideas, they themselves begin to create. This quality of the human spirit brightens our view of the business and labor scene because the problems in ethics are not bigger than our capacity to solve them. ("Our capacity" includes both the human ability and the grace of God.) Only when the God-inspired pump goes dry and our creative impulse turns to apathy do the business and labor issues overwhelm us.

It is important, then, to look for pump primers. These ideas should be brought to the discussion group, posted on the church bulletin board, printed in the Sunday morning bulletin, or included as an item for reading in the order of church service. I have offered only a few pump primers; others will have occurred in your congregation or appeared in church periodicals by the time this book is printed.

The September 28, 1976, issue of *Gospel Herald* printed reports from several congregations participating in a project called JASPA (Jubilee Action Study on Poverty and Affluence). These congregations first studied what Jesus had to say about justice, lifestyle, poverty and affluence issues. Then they moved from Word to deeds. Specific actions in the use of money and other resources by these congregations were shared with readers.

Another church publication, *Christian Living*, has printed a number of articles on family finances, e.g., Joseph Miller, "How Our Family Spends Its Money," August 1975; David Baumgartner, "How Our Family Spends Its Money," December 1975; Adeline Graber, "How Our Family Spends Its Money," May 1976; Susan Ackerman, "Cooling Down Our Lifestyle," October 1976.

The efforts of the Christian Labour Association of Canada should continue to stimulate thinking about employee-employer relationships. CLAC's program and activities are based "on the Christian principles of social justice and love as taught in the Bible." It organizes workers at local, regional, and national levels for "propagating, establishing, and maintaining justice" and "promoting the economic, social, and moral interests of the workers. Its strategy: through practical application of Christian principles, to engage in collective bargaining, mutual aid, and protection." For more information, write to Christian Labour Association of Canada, 100 Rexdale Boulevard, Rexdale, Ontario, Canada.

Those members in your congregation who belong to business and professional organizations will be happy to tell you of new ideas from these associations. I would suggest, in particular, that you contact members of MEDA (Mennonite Economic Development Association), MBA (Mennonite Business Association), and CIBA (Church, Industry, and Business Association). These latter two organizations merged in November 1976 into Mennonite Industry and Business Association (MIBA).

Take the road less traveled by. It shall make all the difference.

Questions for Discussion

1. Describe an occasion when you consciously chose to take a road less traveled by—that is, when you decided to risk and trust a new, strange course of action. What happened?

2. What is the difference between creation and maintenance? Are you by nature a creator or maintainer?

3. To what kind of problems have you devoted most of your maintenance time? To what kind of problems have you devoted most of your creativity?

4. Experiments often fail. Can you cite an example of a new idea in business and labor relations that didn't work out well?

5. Consider the geographical area of your church. Can you identify a section that could, with conscience, imagination, and capital be developed better?

6. Do you think that in some cases the most creative

response is to stop and do nothing? Can one be too action-oriented?

7. Is God a creative person? Explain. Is the devil creaive? Explain this answer, too. How do they differ?

8. If you wanted to pray about creativity what would you say or ask for?

An Activity

Each member should spend 30 minutes recording on a sheet of paper brief answers to these coaxers: Through my participation in these studies—

1. I changed my opinion about . . .
2. I believe more firmly that . . .
3. I am more critical of . . .
4. I have more appreciation for . . .
5. I think our church's first responsibility in business and labor is . . .
6. I wish our discussions would have . . .
7. I want to change my attitudes about . . .

In a final evaluation session, review the responses to these items.

References for Further Study

A. From the Bible (characters in creative encounter)

Jacob (Gen. 32:3-32); Moses (Ex. 4, 5); Solomon (1 Kings 3:5-15); Jeremiah (Jer. 1:4-19); Peter (Acts 10).

B. From church periodicals

J. Winfield Fretz, "Two Mennonite Business Organizations Unite," *The Mennonite*, December 7, 1976.

The JASPA Reports, *Gospel Herald*, September 28, 1976.

Calvin Redekop, "A People in Business and Labour," *Mennonite Brethren Herald,* August 20, 1976.

C. From religious textbooks

J. R. Burkholder and Calvin Redekop, *Kingdom, Cross, and Community* (Herald Press, 1976).

John A. Lapp, *A Dream for America* (Herald Press, 1976).

D. From books about ethics

William T. Greenwood, ed., *Issues in Business and Society* (Houghton Mifflin, 1971).

Notes

Lesson One

1. Samuel Southard, *Ethics for Executives* (Thomas Nelson, 1975), p. 2.
2. Calvin Redekop, "A Christian People in Business/Labor: Reality and Vision," based on a speech delivered to the annual convention of Church, Industry, and Business Association (CIBA) in Wichita, Kansas, November 9, 1975.
3. Abraham H. Maslow, *Toward a Psychology of Being* (Van Nostrand Reinhold 1968), pp.21-43.

Lesson Two

1. Arthur Campbell Ainger. Appears as hymn 605 in *The Mennonite Hymnal.*
2. John Redekop, "Labour Relations Today—A Christian Perspective," a paper delivered at Wilfrid Laurier University, Waterloo, Ontario, April 1975.
3. This summary of attitudes toward material possessions is taken from Guy F. Hershberger, *The Way of the Cross in Human Relations* (Herald Press, 1958). Hershberger relies upon the work of Donald Sommer, "Peter Rideman and Menno Simons on Economics," *Mennonite Quarterly Review* (July 1954) Vol. 28, pp. 205-223.
4. J. C. Wenger, *Even Unto Death* (John Knox, 1961), p. 25.
5. Wenger, *op. cit.*, p. 85.
6. H. S. Bender, quoting Kessler's *Sabbata* (1525) in *The Mennonite Encyclopedia* (Mennonite Publishing House, 1959) Vol. IV, p. 529.

7. J. Winfield Fretz, "Business," *The Mennonite Encyclopedia*, Vol. I, pp. 480, 481.
8. Quoted by J. Howard Kauffman and Leland Harder, *Anabaptists Four Centuries Later* (Herald Press, 1975), p. 291.
9. Kurt Kauenhoven, quoting E. Randt, *The Mennonite Encyclopedia*, Vol. I, p. 41.
10. Kermit Eby, "Let Your Yea Be Yea!" *The Christian Century*, September 14, 1955, reprinted in *Personal Integrity*, Shutte and Steinberg, eds. (Norton, 1961), p. 130.

Lesson Three

1. John Howard Yoder, *The Politics of Jesus* (Eerdmans, 1972), see chapter 8, "Christ and Power."
2. C. Norman Kraus, in lectures to Goshen College faculty at their annual retreat, August 1976.
3. Yoder, *op. cit.*, p. 147.
4. Hendrik Berkhof, *Christ and the Powers* (Herald Press, 1962), p. 30.
5. *Ibid.*, p. 31.
6. Wesley Michaelson, "A Christian Alternative to Power," *Gospel Herald*, February 17, 1976.
7. Southard, *op. cit.*, chapter 1.

Lesson Four

1. Norman R. Weldon, "Strategies for Survival," presented at the Small Business Management Seminar, Goshen College, May 21, 1976.
2. Calvin Redekop, "A Christian People in Business/Labor: Reality and Vision," based on a speech delivered to the annual convention of Church, Industry, and Business Association (CIBA) in Wichita, Kansas, November 9, 1975.
3. "Guilds," *Encyclopaedia Britannica* (1970), Vol. 10, p. 1018.
4. Encyclopedia Americana. *1976 Yearbook*. (Grolier, Inc. 1977) pp. 328-329.
5. John Redekop, "Labour Relations Today—A Christian Perspective," a paper delivered at Wilfrid Laurier University, Waterloo, Ontario, April 1975.
6. For a discussion of eighteenth and nineteenth-century church attitudes toward workers, see Harry W. Flannery, "A Christian Philosophy of Unionism," in *Labor Problems in Christian Perspective*, John Redekop, ed. (Eerdmans, 1972).
7. Adam Smith's *Wealth of Nations* is considered by many to mark

the philosophical birth of laissez-faire capitalism.

8. John Kenneth Galbraith, "The Refined and the Crude," a review of *The Control of Oil* by John M. Blair, in *The New York Review*, February 3, 1977.

9. Sebastian Franck, *Chronica, Zeitbuch und Geschichtbibel* (1531), quoted by Hershberger, *op. cit.*, p. 222.

10. Walter Klaassen, *Anabaptism: Neither Catholic nor Protestant* (Conrad Press, 1973), p. 61.

11. Donald G. Friesen, "The Mennonite Attitude Toward Labour Unions," unpublished paper, Associated Mennonite Biblical Seminaries, May 8, 1975.

12. John Kampen, "Christian Ethics and the Labour Unions," unpublished paper, January 1975, quoted by Donald G. Friesen, *op. cit.*

13. J. Howard Kauffman and Leland Harder, *Anabaptists Four Centuries Later* (Herald Press, 1975), p. 146.

14. John Redekop, "Labour Relations Today—A Christian Perspective," *loc. cit.*

Lesson Five

1. Hershberger, *op. cit.*, p. 62.

2. Dietrich Bonhoeffer, *Ethics* (MacMillan, 1962), pp. 59, 60.

3. *The Journal of John Woolman*, Thomas S. Kepler, ed. (World Publishing, 1954), p. 20.

4. Hershberger, *op. cit.*, see pp. 43-56.

5. Philip Slater, *The Pursuit of Loneliness* (Beacon Press, 1976), pp. 33, 34.

Lesson Six

1. Robert Frost, "The Road Not Taken," *The Poems of Robert Frost* (The Modern Library, 1946), p. 117.

2. Doris Longacre, *More-with-Less Cookbook* (Herald Press, 1976).

3. Philip Slater, *op. cit.*, p. 11.

J. Daniel Hess

Mine is no Horatio Alger story, because I'm still not rich. Just the same, I earned my first coins in modest ways: picking up potatoes, feeding chickens, and stocking store shelves.

I received my formal education at Eastern Mennonite College (BA) and at Syracuse University (PhD in mass communications).

I am neither a manager nor a laborer, but I work hard teaching communications, general studies, and international studies at Goshen College, Goshen, Indiana.

Of the past nine years, we've spent three overseas. From foreign living, I've obtained a perspective on world economics not easy to come by in Indiana. Some of these impressions are recorded in *Vignettes of Spain* (Pinchpenny Press, 1975). On publication date, we will be living in San José, Costa Rica.

Since taking a graduate course in the social and economic effects of advertising, I have consciously and unconsciously gathered material on matters of business/consumer ethics.

An emerging side interest of mine is working as a consultant in intra-institutional communications with businesses and church agencies. I lead employee seminars, analyze message flow, write procedures manuals, and help management clarify public relations issues.

My hobbies are free-lance writing, gardening, reading, and tennis. The most substantial business management experience I've had is balancing the budget for a family of six. My wife, Joy, and I are the parents of Courtney, Gretchen, Ingrid, and Laura.